LR MELVIN

# BETWEEN RAINDROPS

Joanne Stevens Sullivan

# BETWEEN RAINDROPS

*ILLUSTRATIONS by CHIP LAIS*


Penny Avila  Lawson Fusao Inada
Joanne Stevens Sullivan  Vern Rutsala
Anita Lewisohn Hamm  Sam Oakland



Mica Publishing Company
Portland, Oregon

Chapter I. by Penny Avila: *Endangered Species, Air Pollution* are from KALEIDOSCOPE IN A SIFTING OF ASHES, Copyright, Penny Avila, 1982, published by Portland State University; *Downtown My Tuned Piano Leads the Dance, Suddenly the Inner Eye, Flurried by Winter's Wind* are from Ms. Avila's forthcoming book, THE PEACOCK SPREADS HIS TAIL, published by American College, 1985, Madras, India; *The Cascades Near Celilo, Conjectured in Darkness* appeared in The Oregonian's NORTHWEST MAGAZINE; *Arrested on the Scarp, Routine in Offices* appeared in CAVELCADE OF THE ARTS; *Spectator Sport on an Olympic High* was read at the Science Congress of the 1984 Olympics.

Chapter III. by Joanne Stevens Sullivan: *A Yesterday Plan, Mother's Vow, Winter Tree Ghosts, Goodbye, Spring, My Love, In the Midst, Proclamation, Hope* are from ORCHIDS IN THE SAND, Mica, 1984, Copyright by Mica; *The Old Tin Box* appeared in RHAPSODY!, Fall/Winter Edition, 1984; *Mother's Vow* was given an award in 1984 from the Oregon Chapter of American Mothers; *Hell Must Be Fog-Spread* appeared in The Oregonian's NORTHWEST MAGAZINE, 1985; *Winter Tree Ghosts* appeared in the ENTERPRISE COURIER, 1984.

Chapter IV. by Vern Rutsala: *Quest, Paths, Pioneers, By the Willamette, The Journey Begins* are from THE JOURNEY BEGINS, University of Georgia Press, 1976, Copyright, Vern Rutsala; *Sunnyside Road After the War, The Icecold Freight, Moving West, The Mill Back Home, Reedy's Galaxy, Lonely Roads* are from WALKING HOME FOR THE ICEHOUSE, Carnegie-Mellon University Press, 1981, Copyright, Vern Rutsala.

Chapter V. by Anita Lewisohn Hamm: *A Coming Together, Fourth of July Evening, Wintering, John Donne's "Extasie" After Dissection, Pensee, Harbinger, In Case of Drought, Childs Gift, Parts* are from POCKETS OF TIME, Samara Publications, 1982.

Chapter VI. by Sam Oakland: All poems will be appearing in Mr. Oakland's new book, LOVE BLOOMS UNDER THE BLACK UMBRELLAS, Peking, China, 1985.

---



Edited by *Megan Brown*
Book Design by *Joanne Stevens Sullivan*
Illustrations and front cover by *Chip Lais*
Dedication by *Joanne Stevens Sullivan*

---

*First Edition*
*Printing Production by Dean and Marlys Burn*
*Printed by Malloy Lithographing of Ann Arbor, Michigan*
*United States of America*

*Library of Congress Catalog Card Number: 85-60471*
*ISBN 0-931321-01-8/$20.00 Hardback*
*ISBN 0-931321-02-6/$6.95 Paperback*

THIS BOOK IS DEDICATED TO:

Poets

World peace

Continuing dialogue

We
stand side by side
Mind currents
flowing
into
agreement
Each
searching
the heart
for solutions
to continue
standing side by side.

# CONTENTS

## *Chapter I  Windowpanes by Penny Avila*



## *Chapter II  Almost Sun by Lawson Fusao Inada*



## *Chapter III  Dream Clouds by Joanne Stevens Sullivan*

## *Chapter VI Breaking by Sam Oakland*



## *Bibliographies*

## PREFACE

It is the poet, through time, who has kept balance and truth to challenge society's slippage. It is "the poet's work" which libraries want and need and are sometimes denied because of publication costs and popular demand for fiction. For this reason, *BETWEEN RAINDROPS* emerged. This book can be thought of as six mini books. Each chapter is written by an author with individual style — six different lives, loves, emotions, humor, and thought processes. You will find that creativity is alive and thriving. While you are reading, you may notice that the poems are dropped to the base margin — as if sky and space surrounds them. It was done to give you visual freedom, so your mind could travel from structured thought to your unconscious.

Many thanks to Anita Lewisohn Hamm, Penny Avila, Sam Oakland, Vern Rutsala and Lawson Fusao Inada for entering this project. And a special thanks to the artist, Chip Lais, for his many laborious hours with the stippling artwork. Appreciation to Dean and Marlys Burn for printing production, to Revere Graphics for fine film work, and to my editor, Megan Brown.

This book has been exciting from start to finish.

*Joanne Stevens Sullivan*

# Chapter I. WINDOWPANES

*by Penny Avila*

## DOWNTOWN MY TUNED PIANO LEADS THE DANCE

Old when I bought it new, the piano was
carted up thirty-four high-pitched steps
quietly,
rolled through a welcoming door
and settled against the wall.

There, without fingers fingering keys,
music played by a Dorothy long gone
cried up the room.

I play back a different memory:
a small girl's long brown hair glints
like cascading rain in sun,
sparks rebellion like carpal tunnel shocks
through fingers fingering scales
and Bach-Busoni.

Years climbed my back,
the girl left home and discord struck the keys.
The sound of music's gone.

In the recycled school in Old Town
across from Rogers Park
and up from what's left of the Iron Smelter
hard by the river,
a ballet master claps his hands and taps
young rhythms on a polished floor.
Practised fingers cascade over the ivory keys . . .

Sometimes, just inside the door, I'll stand
quietly
watching my piano lead the dance.

## SUDDENLY THE INNER EYE

Through the windowpane

on the world my house affords,
the darkling
dust of settled years,
sunset reflects unbidden graphics
through another window
on another street in a town
I left long ago.

& I can see

like a VCR
the kids almost forgotten
moving/speaking to
events we shared
where a hundred at least
marched down Main Street
on a holiday.

& I can see myself

rained/stained red & white
& blue on Flag Day
cold in a flat bed truck — Columbia
the Gem of the Ocean.

& Lottie Whitford

dancing/dancing just before she shot
up into space when she tripped
on a rock in her yard next door.

& Tom Pezzetti

streaking home with tears & blood
spilling down his sleeve
after the swing my father hung
from the horse chestnut tree
met & matched his practise run
& laid him low as Decker on the turn
in the '84 Olympics.

& now I wonder/ponder

since the one-time shrubs are trees
stretching impossible
greens over the roofline.

& the kids

that kicked-the-can & caterwauled
this part of town drive truck today
or punch computers or legislate
against or for new taxes.

& because

I can't see the neighbors for the trees
the darkling
windowpane sparkles history.

**I'M TRACKWISE BUT HE'S YOUR SON TOO!**

Not my intention. I will not fenderfight.
I am no racing driver, but I'm trackwise;
I know the cars in our garage are chair cars —
which means *those* cars are for *this* family.

I know another piece of news if he does not . . .
we'll soon be in another gas gehenna
bumper/thumping any station with a green flag
for our pit stops. I've ridden car exhausts
for hours for a chance to top our tanks.
Call that my *ooga-ooga-ooga* for no argument!

I am his mother. For sixteen years and more
and more than that I've *been* his mother —
assessing wombtime for the weight it bears.
Why must he be all elbows-past-control at home
and squirrel City Center like a politician?
Our son is into nothing but the Trophy Girls
and what they've got that he can get!

I won't accept 'boys will be boys' as causal,
nor can I let you rate our speedball
from a low of "also ran" to "might make Indy!"
No way, Daddy. If he won't make a slow 360
when my flag is raised, that boy will turn
street jockey talking auto history
and thumbing rides.

I mean this, Daddy, tell our son
— and rev your engine doing it —
no Trophy Girl had better
*ever again*
leave panti-hose in my car!

## THE CASCADES NEAR CELILO

Bosoms pointed at forgotten gods
In a sky stretched gray
The great brown maidens lie
Lengthened
On mountains that cascade
Beside the ledge of shore . . .
Patient
The fivetribe virgins couch
Indifferent to windsong in the gorge
Girding for long gone mornings
That must surely come again
To rise then
Take enchanted forms
To river's edge
And bathe.

## IF THE SEA IS SALT,
## WHY IS A CROOKED LETTER

I see his styled moustache —
stiff hairs that repelled my kiss —
on living faces . . .
bristling and peppered with seasons,
and his breath when he talked
indrawn and hissing as he riddled answers.
Aaron, my father,
channeling words before he sounded off,
sounding between two worlds he knew,
bridging solid stretches of thought.
He would say:

> *You're asking why? I'll trans-e-late:*
> *In Yiddish the word is mer.*
> If I should answer you a truth
> Your *why* is a crooked letter
> In the alphabet you make like this — 'Y' —
> And tell to you another truth . . .
> 'Der Mer Ist Gezaltsen!' I'll trans-e-late.
> It means: The Sea Is Salt!

His italics like mantled gas, inflecting,
and himself, almost lifting with it.
He was a small man, pot-bellied, but prophetic;
his finger underlining logic on new oilcloth
smelling still of Passover ritual
that smothered the *treyfe* in wood.

Dead more than half my life,
his snapshot
against the rail of an Italian liner
bound for the Wailing Wall,
smiles down off *my* wall
his twisted smile that questions:

> Why span extended rights
> In sand, O Israel,
> To bridge the differences
> In hot-blood cousins?
> Why brace catapults
> Against a falling fence,
> Or carry water from a far well
> Leaking from a holey vessel?

Those years ago
my father scored my mind
as breakers score the cliffs
I stand below in Oregon.
I face the East, rockbound on the coast,
walled by water, and my tears are salt.

## IMAGE AND SYNTHESIS

Once when stars were magic
Making a circus of the universe
And I, a child,
Clutching at my trapeze —
It happened that aurora borealis
Made pilgrimage over the east
Dancing maypoles round roman candles
On a small town street —
Lighting the ugliness of Mother Goose,
The waste of bread crumbs in a fairy tale,
Dripping cardinal shades
Over the eaves of houses
Where marriages whored in bed.

That once.

It never came again, and I,
A woman grown,
Forgetting how long the magic lasted,
Forget my mother and my father
Young
And urging me in.

What I remember
With an awesome clarity
About the printed night —
Black sense of blackness
When it was ended
And magic
Spilling stars I caught in my hand.

## ARRESTED ON THE SCARP

I have climbed that mountain
never setting foot in snow
I have tasted sting of cloudcap,
slid the ice
and missed crevasse
I have fingered
the wall of wind
laced golden traceries
on the frosted outcrop
Heard, on the pyramid, people
locked by earth
singing in tongues
out of time
Now on the hogback crouched
where they are lain
to the long wait
I spread my thinning hair
my drying skin
resilient fibers for a cover
until I bivouac.

## CONJECTURED IN DARKNESS

What if wherever green tree-fingers distance
Hill-rising skyward
Dissolves
On a day/in a week/in a year
Under an acid rain
& the fishes bloat belly-up & the whales
Leave the seas & the waters
Beaching/forgetting
Phrased songs humans studied/recorded
Like hieroglyphs on basalt
& the creatures at home in the forests
& the sky birds
Lie death-struck
Become
Fur/bone/hair & the humans & feathers
Fry in the fission the *aficionados*
Play games with, like Pac-Man
As though they were deafened by Science
Were blinded by gene-splicers
Twisted by DNA ripped
Oh what if & what if & what if . . .

## SPECTATOR SPORT ON AN OLYMPIC HIGH

1948 — and the California city cupped in smog
regained a confidence in 'Peace and Plenty'
after global war; Los Angeles reached out
to touch the someones, anyones; hammered
out homes in all directions, spreading
like a Scarlet's petticoats to tempt
the travelers, luring them
to stay and settle in.

1948 — and the city cupped in smog played
host that year to hopefuls vying for place
on Olympic teams. I was *e pluribus unum*
at those tryouts and the night that I recall
so well the stadium was threatened
by oncoming dark, a painted blackness
hovering, engulfing; breathy sound
marked anxious hearts and eyes focused
on bright Decathlon rivals, straining
to finish this grueling second day's five
of ten events and then collapse on waiting
turf . . . benumbed to everything including
WIN . . . LOSE or HOW CLOSE DID I COME!

The arc lights on the field searched out
and found each twist and play of muscle,
trickling sweat, contortion on each striving
face that night of the tryout year;
mostly the dedicated in the stands
were watching this one kid down from Tulare
in the valley, springing up a newly-grafted

vine healed in that good earth, testing
Decathlon strength as a vintner might
a heady mead's bouquet, fermented
for Olympian gods.

In 1948 I had no child
but in my urgent watching *he was mine,*
*and barely seventeen.* I'd urged him on
through 100-meter dash, the broad jump,
shot-put, high jump and 400-meter
on the day before; and now, this day
and night, the 110-hurdles, discus, vault —
screaming till my screams were silenced:
*Do it Bobby! Lift yourself up to the sky*
*above the bar! The sky's there*
*waiting for you! Touch it, Bobby!*
*Up and over!* And the wonder was, he did!
Now the javelin . . . tired kid . . . he seemed
a little boy. I wanted so to shield him
from the pain as his young arms flung
games of ancient Greece at time
and distance into space.

He did that, too.
And now the last, the tenth event —
the 1500 meter on *how much could the kid*
*have in reserve?*
I'd yelled myself completely out of voice
but I had company in every seat
the stadium boasted.

And Bob Mathias down from Tulare,
Stanford bound did win! The Gold in '48 in London,
then the one Decathlon man to bring the Gold
again home from Helsinki, Finland . . . in 1952 . . .
until, in '84, Thompson
skinned it through for England.

Chalk up for me that I was there
watching from the stands,
watching shadowed
seventeen rise
from the games of Greece
to the Forum of the U.S.A.
Senator Robert Bruce Mathias.

Oh yes . . . myself . . . in '51,
I birthed a darling girl
who scraped her knees or nose
or stubbed a toe
at almost every run she made
for puppies or for butterflies.

But she can play the violin.

## FLURRIED BY WINTER'S WIND

Valued at little or less
than Christmas tree popcorn,
I string my worthless days
past where they began.

Unseen instruments play
with innate *heftigkeit;*
the theme and meter sway
until the lullaby.

Unwelcome light points shadow
where there was barrenness
once my bed and pillow
in the scratch of withered grass.

Dead faces, long lost names,
coffins in my mind; and on my tongue
sour cream on greens
we cooked in the color of dawn.

The subway trains still shriek
under Forty-second Street's scene
but I shiver where summer heat
turns to ice in my foolish dream.

Nothing worth saving, I fear,
swirled this against that in the wind;
until somehow a great strand appears
trimming the tree in my mind.

## HEAD IN THE DOORWAY

Peeking, I was almost eight,
more camera than the camera shooting
inside the store. The Maison Chic.
My mother was Madam of the ladies hats
in a corset with eight garters, in a long skirt
and white shirtwaist.

I see her standing at the showcase —
coffin for trimmings: stuffed
bead-eyed birds, cut-steel buckles, silk flowers
feather fancies like on cowboy hats
made then by foreign fingers in the sweatshops
or nights on kitchen tables in the Eastside tenements.
The millinery pretties laid
on shelves of glass — the glass heavy
as my mother's sorrows — heavy as the twins
spinning in her womb . . . a third duty pregnancy
to loveless marriage
custom would not free her from.

My mother designed hats for high society
and for death — she draped fabric on wire shapes
twisted as her life —
pleating black and sorry crepe de chine
like chains about a widow's freedom,
bent over the frame my mother glued
society's moral code to peau de soie.

Six months a widow mourned her fate,
alone, until my mother signaled
liberation with a narrow facing
on the hatbrim — white — symbolic
lightening of grief.

The Merry Widows flaunted purple.
Harpies gossiped months off calendars
while mother listened like a sounding board —
anxious not to lose the trade — and the widow
cast up futures, burbling like a brook in flood . . .
both remembering with no word spoken
how Madam veiled her,
hatted her to weep the office for the dead,
dependent on her oldest child
to guide her to the grave,
so darkly hid was grief behind the veil.

Not breeze-tossed ostrich plumes
in horses' trappings,
nor a costly windowed hearse,
black and velvet draped,
nor half a dozen flower laden carriages
could stem the gossip spilled
by boxom friends probing for news
of the widow from Madam —
in confidence, of course!
"How was the poor dear soul getting over it?
had Madam heard?
and how much did the dear departed
leave the widow?
did she get the house?
the furnishings?
had Madam heard, or did his mother?
and was it true
that Dr. Whatsisface's buggy
was tied up nightly
to the widow's maple tree?"

## ENDANGERED SPECIES

Old women prowl the only supermarket
in the central city, clutch
folded shopping bags like amulets
and lift their worn-down heels just
barely/slowly through the aisles
(as though atoning Vestals in an old disgrace)
searching for signs
that herald "BIG S SPECIALS" on shelves;
buy bones they once gave dogs,
a roll of toilet tissue ripped/rewound,
soap, and last week's bread.

Wind like an angry god whips thinning hair
to doors of buses feeding;
and the old ones' eyes, fading stars
pinpointed in a hurried/harried sky
flickering
as if on cables in the central city
underground
headed for a short.

## ROUTINE IN OFFICES

time is a rubber band
gone out of stretch
no slingshot pull
to ping at rabbits fleeing
a rootless path
meandering by turns on broken buds
dying vegetation seeded by a history
before I tore at birth

time is the sunk bog of seasons
plunked out of weighted skies
tangled in groping vines
strung out and yielding
nothing

I stumble on smells that write large on my mind
turning with my tentative toe
the furry tufts of atavistic animals
crunching on a rip-off

I cling to certain nothings
squashing imagined berries
bruising the fruit at the back
of my tongue

coming at last
to process sly elation
in the basket of my eyes
to pit impermanence of futures
hard against the tug of paper thought
and then I staple the mess
for filing under "L" for logic.

## AIR POLLUTION

Past the Purple Pussycat
the only tenant pays the rent
on time . . .
"Disgrace!" the woman rattles
more than speaks
a certain indignation
in her walk
her cheeks in pants
so tight they underline
what they were meant to cover . . .
agitate
        and stir the air
behind
        with stiff
quotation
            marks.

## FROM THE TOP OF 'A' AVENUE

Coming the final stretch home
A *Shechina* washes the eastern sky
Over Mt. Hood before dusk/before dark
Settles the city. Street lights flicker on
Now here/now there in the surrounding hills.
Someone's fresh-cut grass affords
Great gulps of scented air passing by.

A curious wonder invades my thoughts
Returning from the coast: reminds
The way you peaked your fingers years ago
(Almost as the mountain does the sky)
Beneath our small child's crib-sheet,
Shaping a pyramid of astonishment
Reflected in her eyes
Like promises to keep the faith.

No pine-pocked foothills trace through a mist,
Nor recognition then in the child
That here was father-magic; only wonder
As a mountain rose beneath the blanket
The way we wondered at Paricutin piling up
In a Mexican field, or the passage in the book
That tells how Jacob's ladder lifted.

Do you remember how she looked at you,
That first faith shining? Almost
The way *Shechina* sometimes witnesses
Above the mountain coming home.

# Chapter II. ALMOST SUN

*by Lawson Fusao Inada*

## ALMOST SUN

"Almost Sun" is the moon's song;
the stars, too, can be heard to
lament their lack of recognition.

## SO MUCH FOR THE SUN

The sun just
happened to be
in the right
place at the
right time.

## THE TRIAL OF THE SUN

The sun, of course,
was accused of
polygamy — but what
could they do about it?

## THE SUN'S TRICKERY

Then there was the thing
about the "total eclipse"
which was anything but.

## SUN SEX

The sun, obviously,
is a man.
The only time
he gets
romantic
is when he sets.

## SUN IN THE HILLS

I was lost in the hills.
I had my shadow.

I was lost in the hills.
I found who I was.

## THE COMMERCIAL SUN

The sun promotes itself,
going door-to-door,
promoting everything "solar."

The competition comes back
with "lunar" and "stellar."

## TAKING THINGS AS THEY COME

We take things
as they come.
Sometimes,
they're just
too good
to do without.

This morning,
for one,
I heard this
wondrous,
insistent hum

which was
the living
insistence
of a complete
bumblebee
hovering
on the sill.

Everything
else
was still.
Somehow, it had
entered
my world,

and there
we were,
were we —

in need of
something
to let us be.

I was ready.
It was, too.
And, between
the two of us,
a toothbrush
would do —

to let us
ride outside,
moving as one
through
any doorway,
any corridor,

into the
truest
morning,
into the
lightest
light.

Time passed.
Things came.
Things went.
An era
was the next
event.

For, by the
time
I resumed
my journey,
my task,

I had
cleaned
my teeth,
I had
brushed
my being

with pollen,
with wind,
with petals,
with light.

It was a most
usual
morning.
I've done it
all my life.

## OREGON FOR THE BORED: INTERSTATE 5 REGION

### Introduction

Oregon, too, has its "Tokaido" — its own version of that ancient Japanese highway as immortalized by the artist Hiroshige in his series of prints, "The Fifty-three Stations of the Tokaido." The "Oregon Tokaido" has its own way-stations, its own highlights, its own shrines, and, most certainly, its own history.

Unfortunately, with the advent of the expressway and the accompanying anti-billboard ordinance, much of the true flavor of Oregon is ignored and overlooked by residents and non-residents alike. This handy guide is intended to rectify that.

Written in the time-honored haiku and extended-haiku tradition, things are recorded and presented as is, with only occasional interpolations which are based, nevertheless, on well-documented fact via Nikon and Walkman. Thus, in effect, Oregon tells its own story. Moreover, for convenience, these highlights can be sampled and experienced, with a modicum of imagination, without the reader having to leave the confines of home or a speeding car.

Journey with us now through the "I-5 Corridor," through what was, and is, the "Oregon Tokaido." The first stop is ...

## 1. SISKIYOU REST AREA
## ("Welcome to Oregon: The Status Quo")

A required stop, for
passport inspection;
non-residents must
take the "litterature"
test, and pass through
the "de-Calification
screening area";
non-residents must
make a non-refundable
deposit on the "Oregon
un-resident tarriff";
photo-taking, rock-
removal, and forest-
fire permits are
also issued here
("not available in
stores; fees subject
to current rates
of national inflation");

all permits, however,
are warranteed for
5 years/50,000 miles
by the Les Schwab
Bureau of Management;

upon entry, visitors
are encouraged to
"Re-live the Slide
of '55" ("Siskiyou"
means "moving mountain")
in the new museum,
which also houses
the massive "Oregon
Statue of Limitations."

## 2. ASHLAND

Originally, "Ashram
Origami: Where Everyone
is Holier Than Thou";
"Ash Wednesday Strictly
Enforced"; "America's
Shakespeare Birthplace";
"Bard n' Breakfast";
"Coming Soon: A New
Interchange for
Your Convenience."

## 3. PUC

Former Indian spa
whose sulfur-laden,
healing waters
were pronounced
"puke."

## 4. WEIGH STATION

Former, current,
and future
potlatch site.

## 5. TALENT

Formerly "Talon,"
until the reputed
births, in one year,
in one block, of
Evel Knievel,
Dr. Joyce Brothers,
D.B. Cooper,
Jeb Magruder,
and Bobby Darin

(also, the "step-
brother of Elvis
and Wayne Newton");

Talent is the
"Birthplace of
The Stars."

## 6. PHOENIX

"Graveyard
of The Stars."

## 7. MEDFORD

"Drive Thru
America's First
Drive-Thru";
"Home of the
Annual Paint-
Drying Festival";

"sidewalk tide"
(down in morning,
up at night)
has deceptively
dangerous undertow;

understandably,
residents have
a complex about
being next to
Central Point.

## 8. CENTRAL POINT

Laid out in exact replica
of its sister city, Rome;
"All Roads Lead to C.P.";
considered by many to be
"the exact center of earth";
"Home of America's Only
Known Magnetic Forcefield."

**9. GOLD HILL**

"Pan For Gold at Historic Sutter's Fort — Guaranteed."

**10. NORTH GOLD HILL**

"Whoa! You just Passed North Gold Hill — Bumper Sticker Capital of Oregon."

**11. NEW GOLD HILL**

"Likker n' Lottery!"

**12. OLDE GOLDE HILLE**

"Honest Injun — There's a Heap of Living Here, Podner."

## 13. ROGUE RIVER

"Live! Petrified Forest!";
"Gateway to Crater Lake
on the Scenic Winnemucca-
to-the-Sea Highway!";
"Dance to 'The Donner Party.' "

## 14. GRANTS PASS

"It's the Climate!"

## 15. NORTH/SOUTH GRANTS PASS

"SurvivaLand USA";
"See! The Mason-
Dixon Line! Live!"

## 16. GRANTS PASTURE

"Visit Grant's Tomb!"

### 17. MERLIN

"I Brake for
Dungeons n'
Dragons";

"Ask me
about
the G.E.D.";

"Follow me
to Ye
Roust
n' Joust";

"Scorpio —
and proud
of it!"

### 18. JUMPOFF JOE CREEK

"The Longest Creek in the World";
"J.J.C., including tributaries,
is only 53 feet shorter than
the Amazon, longer than the Nile";
"See! The J.J.C. Crocodile!"

### 19. SUNNY VALLEY

"Site of the Frisbee Massacre";
"Home of Hackysack, Handguns,
and President Harold Stassen";
"U-Pic Herbs and Grasses."

## 20. WOLF CREEK

Formerly, "Transylvania West"
(not for the uninitiated;
rated "PG-13" by tourguides:
"Traveler's Advisory");
the only town in the Americas
with a digital population sign.

## 21. GLENDALE

"Birthplace of John Glen";
many surprises in store
at the "Astral Museum."

## 22. QUINES CREEK

"Bigfoot! Live!";
"Jessie James! Dead!"

## 23. AZALEA

"Home of The Oregon Blues";
an abandoned cabin; a lonely
feeling runs through the ruins;
no waiting; free admission;
"Azalea — some kind of woman."

## 24. CANYONVILLE

"Try Our Red-Eye Special";
"Truckers — You're Welcome";
"Canadian Currency Okay";
"Tour the World's Largest
Senior Citizen Mobile
Retirement Installation."

## 25. RIDDLE

Originally located on the Interstate,
Riddle has been drifting westward since.

## 26. TRI CITY

"The Town
That Time
Forgot,
Remembered,
Reminded";

"Home of Tri-
nity Academy,
the Jackson 3,
the Strike 3
Triangle
Tavern";

"Experience
3 Time Zones
at One Time";

"Future Home
of the Tri-
dent Missile."

### 27. MYRTLE CREEK

"Patrolled."

### 28. ROSEBURG

"Drive-in, Fly-in, Float-in
to America's Only Outdoor/
Indoor All-Adult MovieDome —
Please Stay in Your Vehicles";
"Why Not Try Our Roseburger?";
"Welcome to Africa SafariLand —
No Motorcycles, No Snomobiles —
Please Stay in Your Vehicles."

### 29. NORTH ROSEBURG

"See the World's Smallest
Active Volcano with The
World's Smallest Living
Glacier in The World's
Largest Small Desert";

"Make a Phonecall From
Our Mini-Tabernacle."

**30. EAT 24 HRS**

Not to be confused with
Dine, Munch, Pig Out,
Chow Down, Chatandchew,
Chatandsnack, Gorge,

or All U Can Eat,
or West EAT 24 HRS,
or EAT 23 HRS,
or EAT NOW,

and FAST.

**31. OAKLAND**

"You're Entering
Panther Territory."

**32. RICE HILL**

"Dine Inside the World's Largest
Mobile Home Atop the World's
Tallest Television Satellite Dish."

**33. DRAIN**

"End of
the Oregon
Trail";
"Gateway
to the
Orient";
"Hookups
Available!"

### 34. DIVIDE

"Westernmost
Extension of
The Great
Divide"
(see: Drain).

### 35. COTTAGE GROVE

"Current Resting Place
of Richard M. Nixon";
"Where The Swallows
Go From Capistrano";
"The Cottage Cheese
Center of America."

### 36. GOSHEN

"The First
Capital
of Greater
Oregon
Territory";
"Today's
Scripture
Brought to
You By";
"Coming
Soon!"

**37. CRESWELL**

"The Lost
Capital of
Jefferson."

**38. SPRINGFIELD**

"Visit the Abe Lincoln Cabin";
"Gateway to Rajneeshpuram."

**39. EUGENE**

"Brother City of Gary";
"Home of the Red Guard,
the Avant Guard, and
the Register Guard";

"If It's Ambience —
We've Got It!"

**40. COBURG**

"Yes!"

**41. HARRISBURG**

"Sorry!"

### 42. BROWNSVILLE

"America,
Watch
Us
Grow!";
"E-Z
Off n' On!"

### 43. SHEDD

"Welcome Shriners!"

### 44. ALBANY

"Where the West
Still Survives";
"Visit the Olde
Spanish Emission."

### 45. SALEM

"See Congress
Inaction!";
"Tour America's
Only State
of the Arts
Disposal Site!"

**46. CHEMAWA**

"Tour Oregon's Only
All-Indian School";
"You Are Located
Halfway Between
The Equator and
The 20th Century."

**47. BROOKS**

"The Bottomless Lake";
"The Topless Mountain";
"The Sideless Canyon";
"Topless/Bottomless";
"U Can't Top our Bottom-
less Cup of Coffee."

**48. WOODBURN**

"Forest Fire Capital of The World";
"Walk Thru The Forest Fire Museum"
("currently under re-construction");
"Woodburning Kits for The Family."

**49. WOODBURN DEL NORTE**

"America's Labor Camp";
"Migrant Families 4 Hire";
"Visa/Mastercharge Welcome."

**50. WOODBURNSKI**

"Oregon's Own Russian Reservation!"; "Visit With The 'True Believers!' "; "Witness The Russian Revolution!"

**51. WEST LINN**

"Home of The Annual Columbus Day Storm"; "Re-live Destruction of East, North, South, and Central Linn!"

**52. MILWAUKIE**

"Casket-In-A-Basket — The Bier That Made Milwaukie Famous!"

**53. GREATER PORTLAND AREA: Options**

**a. PALATINE HILL**

"Home of Lewis "Bud" Clark College of the Lite Arts."

**b. THE PORTLAND BRIDGES**

"At any given moment, there are more people on Portland Bridges than in Mesopotamia."

**c. LLOYD CENTER**

"Temporary Resting Place
of Comedian Harold Lloyd";
"Skate Over Harold's Face!"

**d. ALBINA/MT. TABOR**

Former sites of Chinatown I/II;
dynamite testing sites, 1880s.

**e. CHINATOWN III**

"Orders to Go!"

**f. THE CRAB BOWL**

"Seeing is Believing!";
"Severe Tire Damage!"

**g. JAPANTOWN I**

North of Burnside;
formerly adjacent
to Chinatown III.

**h. JAPANTOWN II**

Formerly, and currently,
the Multnomah County Live-
stock Exposition Center.

**i. JANTZEN BEACH**

Formerly, "Chance
Zen Beach" — site
of departure from
Japantown II.

**j. TOMAHAWK ISLAND**

"GypsyLand USA";
"SwapMeet City";
"Gateway to
Celilo Falls."

**k. CHECKPOINT CHARLIE
(OREGON DIVISION OF DEPARTMENTS)**

"You are approaching
Washington — home of
The Trojan Horse and
Mount St. Helens —
It's not too late!
Have you forgotten
anything?"

## Chapter III. *DREAM CLOUDS*

*by Joanne Stevens Sullivan*

## OUT IN THE OPEN

The Oregon sky sheds moisture
filling absorbants
and glistens on salal's bindery.
Bones feel brittle
as ice-coated limb
and pain pulses
in small surges
with constant disposition.
Dampness *Is love's betrayal.*
*A red berry diversion.*
*The sting from holly's spine.*
Snowflakes
quietly laced upon treetops
heaped in drift-waves
appear holier
and more acceptable
than dampness painting rust
on the old iron gate.
Townfolk issue their own Proverb
excuse, "winter rain is spring's gain"
and go about daily chores sprinting
between overhangs.
*I am a seed of winter moisture.*
*A moment in winter's imagery.*
*A raindrop in flight.*
*A dream not yet born.*
My tough shell
moves in and out of raindrops not caring
or trying to find shelter for security.
I laugh at rain, stains, change
neither plan nor direction
and live my life cresting
the tempest day
out in the open.
But, days and days
of dried Payne's Gray
is a vision fogging the mind
and one courting sadness.

## SOLO TALK

Coming from within secure,
moistened walls,
the time was SOLO:
    *crying for warmth,*
    *crying for help,*
    *crying for love.*
Now
in crowded room when other
self-monologue
will not unravel a question,
a glance —
solo is an easy exit from B.S.

It is the smile cast
upon your gaze in denial,
as I move out the door
into exhilaration
between someone
                                and the butterfly.
SOLO
is the SPACE at pew,
counter, park bench,
or cubby hole thinking beyond.
It is the space that swallows
and is held sacred.
SOLO
can absorb a soul
and be the criminal
eluding conversation . . .
stealing the presence
of someone touching.

It can be limelight's victim.
Or, repulsive acupuncture
as friend's needles
prick one's heart.

SOLO
is the stage built,
brick by brick,
for one player. Magnifico!
        It is the magic lantern
of tangential time that must exist.
SOLO
can silence,
be cunning,
cause division,
transform confusion,
dispel peace,
develop solution,
and be the disqualifier
tearing the heart.

INCISE TO HALF
        SO lo
    —BALANCE—
            *Leave room to question*
            *Stand firm against oppression*
            *Acknowledge wrong*

then
DREAM CLOUDS driven by storm
will be calmed.
FEAR will be met HEAD-ON.
Words or gaze will not imprison the mind.
One day,
suddenly, desert light is dark;
a big SOLO comes into focus.
It may carry with it strings of the lyre

playing sad songs
        or
                be swift as East wind.

And one thing is certain,
a pattern not abandoned
will be my exit in SOLO.

## AUSTIN HOT SPRINGS

Autumn foliage presses forward
into the storefront showcase
revealing Joseph's Coat
before the bad guy
hides the garment.
          Suited bodies nestle
in warm mineral water,
raindrops glisten in our hair.
We are bobbers
dodging nature's Jacuzzi
as it spurts boiling spitballs
at our toes and butts.  Cheeks
feel the sting
and our skin turns frosting pink.
          I phantasize
becoming Dancing Faun,
an Indian maiden with Hannah's* face.
My green eyes turn blue as sky pools.
Magic water allows
percentages of favor from Spirit
giving me the strength
of Sitting Bull's squaw.
          We laugh and wallow
in earth fault vents
enjoying unspoiled river water
spilling over Oregon's wilderness.
          My Dancing Faun
rises from sublime,
body healed from special potion,
then returns to being country girl
pulling cowboy boots
over wrinkled feet
under tears
from real Sitting Bull's squaw.

* My grandmother, Hannah Stevens Howard

## IF TRUTH WERE KNOWN

There are corridors in maze
that I have traveled
more than once,
walking to a fifth-beat drum,
grazed by imperfection
and polished by poisoned grit.
Those paths would not be chosen
if chance
would allow walking
the inner
path again. Rather, a new
direction would lead to
creeping barberry,
sharp-edged spade,
plowed field,
apricot,
apple and pear trees
stately lined behind faded barn.
My road would share
Queen Ann's lace,
a fine network
of strings; *Opus Aggrandize* played
by coyote, chickadee and wren.
Today,
I ghost dance with one called
perfection*,
tumbling to upright,
QUIETING
the whirlwind,
slowly
working toward merging with eventuality.

* God

## I WAS A BLADE OF GRASS

When child of five,
I became
as blade of grass,
ocean shifting,
weaving in the wind;
camouflage from gold to brown
in field of wild tobacco, daisies
and laced ladies standing tall.
Hiding with the snakes,
staying close to ground,
all were the enemy that day.
Curled small in sun,
with stick-tied bag,
eating peanut butter/jelly slices
and red apple snitched
from Mama's kitchen.
Never, never,
would my legs
cross
threshold
back to cell-tight rooms.
The grass was home.
So lovely . . . for two whole hours.
Button-eyed bugs with multiples
of legs, long antennas signaling
friends, hoppin' hoppers paraded by,
and birds in angularity
sounded for slippery worms —
all became dim under clouded sky.
Then home
my short legs ran.
Mama never knew my secret.

I was a blade of grass
growing in the sun.

## MY TENTH TOE IS JEWISH

Pan flutes
have played
sad melodies before
drifting through reeded banks
echoing
through olive branches
across
sand-blown tapestry
of stones
Hidden
from memory
are nomadic tales
of tribes in Exodus
dispersion
of climbing ghetto
walls to freedom
Hidden
from memory
are ancient songs
kosher food
joking ways
and cultural verbiage
The
old picture
revealed secrets
(once shrouded by deception)
A deep craving
for pastrami on rye
has been resolved
my tenth toe is Jewish

## A YESTERDAY PLAN

Once, I walked the Ditchrider's Road
stumbling over bulging furrows
startling birds in awkward surprise
and coyotes sneaking by
after nighttime blues.

I can still feel hawk eyes peering
into my soul
and wonder why I left absorption
for a city intimidated,
surrounded by noise.

Why did I leave
the creeping purple spread
made up from seeds
husked in last winter's ice,
or Baby's Breath,
wild and white,
hugging
the Columbia Southern's wandering lip,
or mint fields catching
the breeze to my nose?
Why did I leave sand avenues
lined with squirrel soldiers
stealing enemy supplies,
or sagebrush shading insectland,
and my guardsmen, the birds?

Why did I leave nine mountains
towering at my gate
and the pink/tangarine Sunday sky?

A yesterday plan,
a yesterday desert,
by a yesterday poet —
is a luminous seed
waiting to sprout again.

## YOU LEFT
## TRAILING RED-FLARED SKIES

Words written
inside my mind
were tendered
in your eyes,
sawgrass danced
in wind-song hymns
and tide bellows
spread strings of foam paths
in sea horse currents.
Seagulls
were drifting fans
crying calls
of haunting fear.
Then . . . you were the seagull
drifting in wind sails,
silently
crying out in terror
and my heart crested
at your peak
as your soul slipped
into a foreign world.
You left
trailing red-flared skies
touching darkness
in quiet observation
and hope followed you to hell.

I held court one day,
as Apollo rode the sun away
and found you guilty
of being the tracker
who pierced my lonely heart.

## GROWING, GOING

Mirror's reflection warned
that eating fantasy for breakfast
and dining on criticism for dinner
has chequered
threads and exposed the road
to forgotten.

Emerald eyes have faded
into muddy green,
shades of the Trask River
winding over Tillamook pastures.
Hands are wrinkling
and creaking with knotty joints.
Small freckled saucers dot
brownsugar/sandpaper skin.
Heartbeats thump in sync,
but the mind runs races
with a '40 Ford.
                    Jokes spice
the day.
                    Son says,
"how high's the bullshit, Mama."

                    And I say,
"ankle deep and ris'in."

When too much agitation ruffles
up my aisle,
old Leatherhide pulls up,
up and away
                and is GONE.

**STALKING BEAR**

Perhaps one day
you may wander through hills
of Southern Oregon's pastoral
paradise.

*Land where Indians stood*
*Hawk's watchful eye*
*Patient in thorough research*
*Combat/fear in readiness.*

Don't walk too far and enter
Stalking Bear's sanctum,
where tall, powerful plants
grow more important than
human life. From rock precipice
beside the hissing sun-bather,
Four-eyes observes trees,
canyons, trout streams,
bottoms . . .
disallowing excuses for
treading on the land — his finger
squeezes trigger.

If fate should score one day,
and fireballs devastate the land,
and perchance,
Stalking Bear, armed with his
fireball device, survives . . . .
the dead will at last
be free.

## THE OLD TIN BOX

Closet cleaning met emotion
one autumn day,
as clutter was rearranged.
Hiding beneath blue jeans,
a thickness from my heart,
the old tin box held faded dreams.
The contents issued tears,
children's paper kisses,
tainted pain
and patches
of assorted color.
Back then,
I walked rainbows to the sun
and caught midnight moonbeams
on silken wind
with a vagabond love.
Destiny was a prism
shining inside my head,
and reality,
the warrior walking a quarrelsome road.
Years of silent beginnings
have turned from piety
into a spirit charged
with dangling words — unafraid of fate.

The box held Khayyam's writing
*And this was all the harvest*
*that I reap'd — I came like water*
*and like wind I go.*
And the harvest I have reap'd
are five fine souls
and the words contained
in the old tin box.

## SKY KING

Hum, hum,
descender, ascender,
weight of a dime.
Tiny self cannot hop
                    or walk
upon the ground.
                    Destiny
is to skate upon
                    air
fanning tiny wings
as a Las Vegas card shuffler
or a band's twirling majorette.
Swordbill dips
into flower nectar,
then whirs away to clutch,
as baby hummers await,
hatched from pea-size eggs.

Sky King,
pilot of the sky,
dancing tarantella to the rain,
one day you may enter
dream world
pushing cool air against my face
on a hot sultry night.
Hum, hum.

## THE ARTIST AND THE POET

Friends we are,
the artist and the poet,
gazing at the butterfly,
hurling through eccentric
tunnels — halved
in whole symmetry.

We ride rapturous currents
in canary sunlight
and work through
night depressions
into quiet dawn
unable to sleep.
We climb stairways of growth,
tumble,
            then hold
the trapeze once again.
We drink nature's moselle
articulating cadence
on canvas and with pen,
finalize the ending stroke
and glide from mind swirls,
silently,
while energy rests
recharging.

Then we wait

for a renaissance to begin.

## ALTORESCO, PUT THE KETTLE ON

It's time to sip the rosehip tea,
discuss
          preadventurous tales
pressed inside
and how about fixing
your famous cucumber soup?

I will bring five
scarlet hollyhock seeds,
one orange spider dahlia,
a garage sale book on
                    beekeeping
that cost me fifty cents,
and one home canned jar
of dill pickles
               in exchange.

## MOTHER'S VOW

A vow was born
deep inside my mind:
"I shall love, honor, respect
this small child until maturity.
From that moment,
I shall clip dependence
and stand on the perimeter
waiting
for gales that may bring
unforeseen misfortune.
Then my hand will reach out
lifting the spirit toward truth
and into my pocketbook of wealth
to feed this child's life
with words passed down
from another generation."

**MOTHER TREE**

I
HAVE
BIG
SHOULDERS
SHEDDING RAINDROPS
FALLING
&
I SHELTER SMALL FRIENDS CALLING
HIDE
THE TRAVELING
MIDNIGHT RAIDER/RIDER
& SOME FRIENDS CLIMBING HIGHER &

I UMBRELLA • • TINY FLOWERS

R
E
S
T
I
N
G

— UNDERNEATH ON SACRED GROUND —

## WINTER TREE GHOSTS

Tree ghosts filter
over winter's bare tentacles,
tracing skeleton's refinery,
chasing curved shadows
winding
on grey-etched lichen filigree,
then retreating into a nebulous sky.

Tree ghosts ride the rain,
hiding in foggy bogs,
mossy swamps and messy marshes
in decaying/hollowed stump
hideaways,
waiting to haunt
a lonesome, shivering soul.

Those fleeting diaphanous ghosts
play games with birds,
squeezing into tight corners
of territorial camps,
whishing through branches,
swaying old trees with ghostly
lullabies.
Riding in a gust of wind,
ruffling/hustling, shaking
woodland playgrounds,
they find only firs and pines
to hopscotch through
and fern fronds to dust.

Tree ghosts are biding time
until Flora visits some sunshiny day
in her new bridal gown;
then spider webs will fill
with careless winter tree ghosts.

## GOODBYE

Old bare bones,
temporary occupant,
your time is finished
for another year.
Morning sunshine coaxed
tiny buds into fluffy vestment
crowning wildflowers to reign.
Today, when I looked out
to the distant hills,
there was a hint of mustard
painted over you.

Putting on redress
gives me hope,
after living through your
                                        wailing
temper
            tantrums
and
looking at your
old bare bones all winter.

## SPRING, MY LOVE

Old pages have been written,
some beautiful,
and some harboring
under-the-cover blues.
An opened hearth allows
light to filter through strands
                                        of memory
that once held together
another time
                    another place.
A yellow daffodil
                        lived
by the trunk
of an old gnarled tree
shifting in the wind
as rain pattered footsteps
                                        on spring
and garnishment
trickled on her garment.
We sang songs in playful harmony,
philosophized of love (the promise
of tranquility)
and hoped spring would never leave again.

## WHILE MAKING LOVE

Touching the covering
of his long straight legs,
I play cops and feels
and ride high tide
with playful energy.

Intellect wars
with eroticism —
juggling
a subconscious flutter.
The whole of me
rides the new wave
eclipsing biology;
cresting thin mountain air,
masterminding
treacherous phrases.
                    Truth comes, hovering.
Tiger meets Lion
at love lane exit
and all that I am
remains married
to this damn pen
as a poem
squeezes into existence.

## IN THE MIDST

In the midst
of earth's mildew,
        poverty,
your profile has become
        sweet jasmine
erasing past bitters.

## PROCLAMATION

Emancipation is a full feeling
leading to many places
and one that I will never release
from my new life.
It's with me as the sun
lazily breaks over the hill,
until it looks for Japan
in the West.
It is thickly spread
over my body
covering most places,
yet, a bit of dependence
sneaks through
when I am with you.

## HOPE

Hope is the breeze
fluttering in the soul
stirring unsettled
promises,
clothed in angel wings
to lighten the load.

## HELL MUST BE FOG-SPREAD

Hell must be the cake
iced with fog-spread;
each step slicing
into unknown isolation,
consuming sounds
thoughts
and the brightness
of one's heart.

## THE WHITE VELVET LAST EXPRESS

Truth
is hidden
from thirsting souls;
thin-coated with delay,
scourged,
sliced,
and shut away
in closet.
Yet,
the hero riding
the white velvet last express
arrives
at the mind on time
handing over
truth
for the
final decision.

# *CHAPTER IV. LONELY ROADS*

*by Vern Rutsala*

## BY THE WILLAMETTE

All day the frantic
mill shouted
wooden tallness
down: Every
tree shall be
a conscript
to the cause
of paper!
But now the slow
rumor of a tug
slides by;
log rafts
huddle in dozing
schools
nibbling shore;
a lone canoe
cuts the surface
like a paperknife
scattering moonlight;
and downstream
the Ferris wheel
in the park slowly
mills the night.

## THE MILL BACK HOME

Logs drowse in the pond
Dreaming of their heroes
Alligator and crocodile

## REEDY'S GALAXY

On summer nights
The south wall
Of Tim Reedy's
Tarpaper shack
Looked like a sky
Full of stars
Lamplight
Shining through
The countless
Tiny holes
He put there
Killing flies
With his silver .22

## QUEST

Driven like a fugitive through splintered shadows
I searched all night
for my old houses —
for the other life, the buried one, the lost vanished life.

Where did it live? What was its address?

I worked my way down cold alleys
numbly as an old man threading a needle;
I crossed at the dangerous corners
and passed empty schoolyards
guarded by cyclone fences,
a drone behind slate windows.

Once we dreamed and woke to another dream:
fishflutter of leaves, sun throbbing dust awake,
the warm stone's shape invented by our fingers.

I entered a door and my hand remembered
a loose bolt, my foot nudged a cracked tile alive
and slid familiar as a broom over the worn threshold.
Again I met the mysteries of cupboards, the prim necks
    of faucets,
the frozen mirror thawed for me.

Upstairs I saw a ceiling light with its knotted string
    like a spider.
I saw the bed and heard the music of its springs again.
Once touched each object shivered.
They pulsed with my old life, these blind witnesses.

**PATHS**

Walking alone on a strange street
I feel an old excitement,
a stirring like those car trips
in childhood that promised
another life, a new school
of echoes, the dull cargo
of the fool thrown overboard
for good: An old car climbs
the grade on Cabbage Hill
coughing steam, tires tender
as balloons. I remember
the knocking motor and all
around me the great silence
of held breath before we
breathed the icy summit's view.
The freight of memory
lumbers with me now down
all that twisting altitude.
My cardboard house folds up.
I am on the path again
that shows you how to lose.
Ozone's lost taste on the air,
no wind, no stir in the leaves
fears become eyes, an eye
for each weeping knothole,
eyes on my skin like kisses.
Once there were rumors
of dead grandfathers — muffled
voices in another room —
and whispers of others lost
in the woods, smothered bones
turned to twigs overnight.
I felt the force of the woods —
ferns winked starvation's eyes

and the cougar of the dark
padded close, huge yet so
delicate no twig broke.
The cat is always there
in the forest thick as sleep
near the path that leads
to cold kitchens. Deeper still
I remember the dirt road that led
to the old farm and how the car
bucked and rattled like a milktruck
over potholes, the farmhouse
rising and falling, pines dancing
the sky jagged. I waited
for the plank bridge. It seemed
only an armload of kindling
thrown over the ditch deep
with brown water, boards warped
and split and thin as lath to
let us drown. But I knew
that if we fell it would be
farther, not just into brown water,
but farther, deeper, darker,
colder than water.

## PIONEERS

Summer surrounds us tonight.
Leaves are thick on the trees,
the neighborhood quiet, the only
sounds echoes. The streetlight
burns, lynched to its pole
and traffic dwindles to the few
late drunks squinting to keep
curves out of the road.

We are in another house
but darkness is the same old pool
we fish our madness from.
It follows us like a stray
and makes me think of all
the places we've lived, gone now,
torn down, washed loose by floods,
picked up and moved at night

to other sites as if someone were
removing evidence, burning bridges.
The vacancy of those houses clutches
tighter than summer, those rooms
emptied of our signs, stations
on a trail that goes one way.
Our lives are engraved with fingerprints
on old magazines, dented pots,

the dog-eared mystery stories left behind.

## SUNNYSIDE ROAD AFTER THE WAR

Ancient flypaper curls in winter
light and I drive back
over all those gravel roads
through dead farms, land sucked dry,
scorched grass the pale
memory of crops. I hear guitars,
amplifiers tuned high,
as toothless singers
cry of careless
love and wildwood flowers.
I remember the oily windows
blurring amber as I fell asleep.
I fall asleep that way again
and hear the whooping
name of that parched summer,
boozed yodels daring
the night to end.
And again they look for jobs,
look on all the wrong streets,
knock on all the wrong doors
and wind up in the sick
light of waterfront bars.
What the hell, you
can always use a shovel
for the county.
August's fires died, rain
filled ditches, their clunkers
wouldn't start, strings broke.
They sat in their shacks, the war
was over, they strummed, caught colds
and watched the stiff brims
of their beautiful hats
go gray and limp.

## THE JOURNEY BEGINS

Now they are loading the old Ford in the evening, taking too much luggage,
too much fried chicken in paper sacks, lost
even before leaving the muddy driveway.
With great care they jammed dirty shirts and underwear in the cracked suitcase,
everyone's clothes together, rank and wrinkled, the flanks
of the case already sprung, the lock losing its hold slowly.
Cardboard cartons filled with rusty towels, a half box of cereal,
the iron with the frayed cord go into the back seat
with army blankets and the squat thermos, spout dripping.

The old man sits very still on a kitchen chair while the women work.
His wife, near seventy, sighs and trembles
afraid of highway curves — blowouts hover on the road,
some vast clock figures collisions, fiery breakdowns coil
under the old car's hood. All afternoon she
travelled that long highway, conjuring each dangerous inch,
seeing guardrails spring open like gates
and the flimsy car soar and bounce down ravines
so deep no one has seen the bottom.

The old couple know only that their fat daughter has come
to rescue them from his sickness, its confusion, its haze
around them like woodsmoke.
She drove five-hundred miles fueled by her mother's hysteria:
He was dying but still stumbled into town to drink,
swollen hands like mittens around a shot glass.
Drunk, he beat those big hands blue on the woodshed door.
Sober, he said the bar was there to keep him
from sitting like some old woman eating toothless bread and milk
with a baby's spoon hooked around his thumb.

He staggered home by moonlight, screaming through jackpine
for Bud and Ed, both dead twenty years,
to wake up and have a goddamn drink.
So his daughter — forty-five, three hundred pounds —
drove all night, losing count of flats,
splashing water into steam on the radiator.
Even now as they load the car she eats left-overs.
Her hands always seem greasy, the skin around her mouth
   glistens
and her lips shine as if she had just licked them
before having a picture taken.
You were always such a pretty girl, her mother says. So pretty.

The car sags with its burdens, mud high on the fenders like a
   watermark,
one headlight squinting blindly through the gloom.
The suitcase is now loosely tied on the trunk with
   clothesline —
the daughter counting more on balance than tension
in the line to hold it there. It is her way.
Springs lurch as they get in, the old man settling his brittleness
among blankets and boxes in the back.
Now fear of the road becomes worry over the house:
for the old woman every shingle becomes tinder,
every rafter flammable as balsa wood.

They set out in the dark along a dirt road, a blizzard of dust
around them from a passing logging truck.
Soon the old man sleeps.
His daughter counts his breaths in the rearview mirror.
The old woman winces at every branch that looms swiftly
like an enormous hawk above the car,
scrapes and thumps a claw once and is gone.
The car creeps and whines until they reach the cool blacktop,
suddenly free as skaters on the interstate.
But the wrong turn has waited patiently all day
and they take it gracefully, relaxing on the level road.
The old woman even hums and forgets fire.

They drive on, their lone map lost in a sack of fried chicken,
grease spots forming on it slowly, darkening the land.
Chainsmoking and swearing the daughter keeps steering north,
trying somehow to lean her bulk toward the West,
but the road refuses and they go on and on
as the dark smothers the car
and the blazing white hospital sheets recede with each
wheezing mile the old man breathes away.

## THE ICECOLD FREIGHT

**for Kathe**

Thirsty, I turn the radio on
letting noise fill my gaps —
a country music whine,
that studs and shiplap sound,
that skeleton of feeling,
old nails pulled from boards.
Old man, father, whatever
your name, I swim
back through dust
and wood chips, back
to the summer we built
a house together and beyond,
deeper, the time you grew
a beard. I remember
the straight razor slicing
your chin. I remember
the scar you carried
to death.
Tonight
I want everything in —
frost slowing forming
on the car roof
as if the streetlight
scattered a kind of talcum;
my homemade valentine
dangling from the light cord;
and the undertaker's breath,
pre-sweetened, his ashtray filled
with paperclips.
Coffee boils,
I sit back and drink
its darkness, hard times
falling with the ice.

We're taking our own
medicine again, those small
bitter pills doled out
by persimmon-faced
nurses. Hard times
music like that throb
you carried all your life,
that Depression war wound —
how the world went
cold and gray, how it
would go that way again.
You knew that icecold
freight was on the way
and knowing made you gunshy
and careful with a hammer.
There were no second chances,
a nail gone was
a nail spent.
                    I listen now
to truck stop
music getting everything
in, singing of lost
farms and the dead —
echoes, gristle music.
With your wound you
took your time that
summer. I hated
slowness and every board.

Victim of the miter box
you checked and checked,
carpenter's pencil scrawling
over every two-by-four,
testing each deceptive
number. You thought
nature lied, in cahoots
with politics. Nothing should be
easy and every calculation
must be triple-checked.
In the way and useless,
despising the dry ground,
I longed for trips
to the little store for cokes
and cupcakes and slow talk
in the cool interior
with the crazy owner.
But you kept at it
and slowly a house
rose from nothingness.
The music
goes on, on the edge —
like Humbird and Wiebe
in their shacks that summer,
guitars filling dusty
air with song. They played
and played and sometimes
brought over a beer
and helped lift the rafters,
half drunk but willing.

The war was over, jobs
were hard to find
and the icecold freight
churned through those
summer fields. But
the house rose, bit by bit —
almost finished when
we moved in, tarpaper
and half a floor.
That winter we froze
and I hated it
but tried to swear
and cough like you,
tried to bang around
the kitchen mornings
before school — and played
football hard, knowing nothing
was easy.
In the music
I hear your saw
whine, sense your tack hammer
on the roof in little
beats. Frost is gone,
rain falls the way it did
that year when the oil heater
never gave enough heat
and I ran to the kitchen
to get dressed.
Now rain eases, ghost blossoms
unclench in strangeness.

I feel the old chill,
the hard times throb.
The neighborhood was desolate —
shacks and tents and not
a tree in sight. Like
the music Wiebe and Humbird
twanged every night
until I went to sleep.
Ancient summer uncovers
ancient summer — your
beard, your razor cut,
your scar — memory
traveling back and forth,
pacing through another rain
in hipboots and galoshes.
Buds nudge and die
in the cold, the city lops trees
to stumps, and that far-off
house endures the weather
still, held up with nails
my irritation pounded
home.
Monument enough for you —
worried into being by
your flat pencil and your
curses, a place to live,
no shrine. I learned this
and then forgot and now
it comes back: The cutting board,
the thumbed book, the worn
furniture speak our lives to us.

And I wonder if
the handmade backboard you
put up still stands.
The net shredded off
the hoop the first year
but I used it hard,
working on my left hand
hour after hour. You signed
and swore that scarecrow
structure up as well — for me —
another monument of use
and the need to learn
Joe Fulks' jump shot.
And for a while we kept
the icy freight off
that street. It was music
and shacks and hot
summers, football and baskets.
The radio says it's lonely
time and I believe it.
The radio sobs and whimpers,
tough guys ground
to jelly. They know, they know.
With Wiebe and Humbird
I switch to wine, fed up
with unemployment checks
and coffee. Ghost trees
haunt the neighborhood. Money
for a sixpack turns up
under a flat rock. Hope
tunes our strings and pays
light bills. But we
wake to tarpaper and tents,
to empty cupboards
and jobs likely
as a royal flush.

The icecold
freight warms up nearby
and its diesel fouls
our summer, the bad news
only war can cure.
The freight snorts and paws
like a bull, needing us.
And Truman, you said, shuffling
his deck finds some action
in Korea, and the summers
disappear. A brother of the freight
scattering dollars pulls in,
wheezing red steam. We
still live with that lukewarm
freight that mulches
everything. Humbird and
Wiebe and I listen to your
music, remembering. The old
house turns monument
and lost, and father,
I
see you in your railed bed.

I trim your fingernails —
there's nothing else to do.
Your hands are thin, I.D.
bracelet so loose on your wrist.
We built a house together!
The radio sings lugubrious —
I go all the way back again,
touch that summer, that scar,
vow a beard no matter what,
dream guitars and sun
dream hammers and studs,
dream that house from nothingness
again — our monument,
the one I hated every inch of,
the one we built together.

## THE OTHER ROAD

Where the asphalt runs off the page
I begin

At the county line
The road buckles with pain

Its shape dictated in spring
By wheels by boots

By whatever can gouge
With summer it sets

Like a twisted ribbon of sculpture
Delivering up the potholes

Earned last winter
This is our road

The one we're told to take
They make it tough

But we expect nothing easy
None of those humming interstates

Without a seam
None of those cobblestones

Set like jewels
This is our road

## GRAVEL, ROADS, FATHERS, IDAHO, HOBOS, MEMORY

We move slowly now over gravel,
the last hint we've had of roads
in this long search for our fathers.
We hope this place is Idaho
as we were told by hobos
so far back in our memory

it's nearly lost. Or is this memory
we touch and only think it's gravel,
our path more lost than any hobo's?
Perhaps we've followed too many roads
as imaginary as the place called Idaho
where they said we would discover fathers.

But still we are without fathers
except those fading images in memory
who invented this wilderness of Idaho.
Soon enough we'll eat the gravel,
soon enough we'll abandon roads
and jungle-up forever with the hobos.

Or do we dream the hobos
as we dream our lost fathers,
night after night along these roads?
There is something in our blood, a memory
grinding like gears to produce this gravel
we scatter like seeds all over Idaho.

## LONELY ROADS

**for Joan**

What roads we followed, what interstates
of discontent, needle paths, pavements
pounded to flour to reach this room!
We trace them back tonight,
the surgical scar of that railroad,
a blue line of gravel through the hills.
We follow them all finding some tangled
as string in old drawers, unraveling
with ancient scarves, spread out
in our wrinkled palms, that relief
map of our lives. What dreams
brought us here? What fissures
have they crawled, what visions
of black light in the deepest fathoms
of our sleep? We trace them tonight,
each following a different route.
You go where you must —
the lonely Greyhound, five days
of cheese sandwiches, the half a house
where your childhood lives.
I move along the Columbia,
split off toward Ontario, Weiser, climbing
away from flat heat, dinosaur hills.
And as always New Meadows sleeps
except for the single light at the depot
left on for the bugs. Climbing
I uncover old anticipations like road signs,
catch that old taste of air, thin and clear,
the old house taking shape room by room,
the town rising around me
as I climb the stairs to you
flagging down your lonely Greyhound.

# Chapter V. MIRACLES OF RAIN

*by Anita Lewisohn Hamm*

## CONTRASTS

I cannot hear
what you say
for the crashing of rain
slanting its spears
against the south windows.

I would like to say,
"Remember
the wild strawberries
gleaming garnet
after a summer rain?"
You thought somehow
the strawberries
were a metaphor for me —
your green salad love —
or did I just think
you thought that?

But you
cannot hear what I say
because
of the crashing of rain
and the slanting
of your thoughts
at an oblique angle.

## BLUE RAIN

Where are you
this four o'clock afternoon
when the rain is falling
in great sheets?
Where are you
when I'm couched
in a wool coverlet
of rejection,
alone?
Are you
also in a cave,
taking your ease
in dim lit cacophony?

My music,
my flowers,
my books
do not interest you.
I will stir
my solitary cup of "instant"
and pretend
I'm hosting another lover

of rain.

## A COMING TOGETHER

Today we made poetry
which is something
like making love.

A high bright fire
sings in the blood,
touching off radiance.

Small rainbows
glance
off words.

Small arcs are struck
from our thoughts
as we made a weld

fragile
but enduring.

## WONDER

In a plumeria afternoon
we are crowned
with warm rain.
Our sandaled feet
are mired
beside orchids
and wild ginger.
This miracle
of raindrop
may have seen
the Taj Mahal,
China's Great Wall,
or a pagoda palace
before falling here
and telling
its small warm story.

## FOR A COLLECTOR

of weather there are splendored rains:

A night rain shimmers with color
on a city street, marquees ablaze
and signs, however prosaic,
lend radiance to long ribboned
reflections on pointe.

There are quick spring rains
that turn a ribbon of asphalt
into blinding silver when the sun
comes out. Rains make blue puddles
with dark pencil outline.

And then there is a whispering rain
that presses spilled red maple leaves
on a cement walk, the steady
relentless pressure bleeding
red juices from dead cells.

There is the rain of diagonal pen
strokes by the master Hokusai
on a museum wall: Coolies hunch over as
they make their tortuous way —
a million knife edges against resisting
flesh in rain-and-wind-soaked shirts.

There is a freezing rain encasing
early-set camellia buds in crystal.
It enters the capillaries of pines
that explode like rifles through the night.
Rain-ice hangs a fringe of gleaming
stilletos over windows and eaves.

## DIAMONDS

Cups of fresh wood sorrel
hold rain jewels
in their dimples.
We beggars
forget our needs
and appraise
the transient hoard
with pleasure.
Ah, rain.

## FOURTH OF JULY EVENING

A burst of emerald stars spring to gold,
fountains of red and amberescent flow,
a spray, cyannic blues and lavenders,
arpeggios made visual and chords
crash upon the sight, a legend
written on the velvet night expanse,
and then no trace until the year wheels
round again.
Thunder drums and rain descends.

## WINTERING

Listen!
Wild poetry of wind
                                        in firs.
Picture
the slow denuding
of branches.
Hear the staccato of rain
on dead leaves.
Tomorrow
pale amber
will sift the fog
and light up brown fungi
where flowers grew.
Wild poetry-of-wind
                                        in firs.

Listen!

## JOHN DONNE'S "EXTASIE" AFTER DISSECTION

It lay upon the page palpable
in its loveliness, a thing
of grace, with glints of gold
glancing in the light.

But we must tear
the unity from
its metonymy.
Must separate
the trochees
from the dactyls
and see where falls
the anapest.
Ah, sad,
the scansion does not fit
iambics of footfalls,
and where is
the internal rhyme?
And could
the poet have had in mind
a deep
psychological intention
when he wrote
about a pregnant bank
of violets swollen
with spring rain?

The poem lay back upon the page —
a tattered thing — robbed of grace,
like roses broken and strewn.
Must a lovely lyric always end like this?

**PENSEE**

I took the rain
into my thoughts,

counted the rings
it dropped into the pool
below the bridge.

It spoke a gentle patter —
recitative to browning
leaves meshing the path.
It called to some brooding
sense in me that said,
"Winter is on the way."

## HARBINGER

Year after year
he stands in rain or sun,
his green and white umbrella
anchored to the earth.

He sells the spring in cans
of daffodils, for fifty cents.

## THE CLEANSING

The dust settles
in drifts.
A pregnant stillness
pervades the world.
Thunder comes in bass chords.
Lightning flashes
and burns a tree.
The rain comes quietly.
Like tears.

I weep
for a tree.
It stands charred for decades.
In time it will lose
its charcoal
and reveal its decaying
brown heart.
Its dust runs away
in rivulets to new drifts.

## IN CASE OF DROUGHT

"Send my roots rain,"
Gerard Manley Hopkins
begged abjectly.

We, too, petition
the starlight
to send flowers of snow
to a starved mountain
so that fawn lilies
once again
may emerge
pristinely
from the melt
to cover the slopes
with delicate fires.

Send *all* roots rain.

## ECCLESIASTES REVISITED

There is a rain for walking,
a rain for pulling weeds,
a rain for turning the earth
before dahlia-planting time.

There is a rain for sowing seed,
for storytelling in candlelight.
There is a rain for watching
behind a drenched windowpane.

There is a rain for listening
at winter solstice, when lying
in bed luxuriating in the year's
longest night. Shhh—

Do we hear
a gentle gurgle in the gutters
or is it
the silent
coursing of our own blood?

## 'TIS THE SEASON

My winter
is a lilac scrim
misting the hills.
It is puffy brown mushrooms
quietly decomposing the roots
of my cedar tree.
It is a quickening of wind
in tall firs.
And rain.
A residue of maple leaves
drifting between spreading
tentacles of ivy and vinca.

My winter
is gray crustose lichen
adorning branches, lush moss
in the lawn which cushions
an occasional footfall of towhees.
My winter
is the winter wren
who sings the longest song,
a book I cannot put down until
I've drained
its essence
drop by drop.

My winter
is the cloistering
happiness of snow
and letters from my loves.
My winter
is filled with subtleties,
soft shadings,
and music
enough to soothe the soul.

## SEQUESTERED

Umbrellas bloom
like pansies
in soft jets of rain.
Lovers
under a lilac umbrella
whisper and laugh
in this small circular
shape of privacy.

Their shared intimacy
has no sharp edges —
only the spokes
that give definition
to the silk
above their heads.
They tilt the umbel
against the wind in joy.
They steer a path
into the elements
while pedestrians
scramble out of their way.
The shelter wraps
them in a cocoon
that only lovers
and silk worms know.

## AGAINST A TIME LINE

Right as rain,
we used to say.
A rain for everything.

Like a rain
for keeping albums,
collecting
motley snapshots of the dead,
the nearly dead
and the vibrant living,
framing them
in continuity of pages
between green covers.

Nineteenth century babies
in lace
grin at us
with the same fixed sweetness
as today's babies.

Are they stirring
in their graves
as we shuffle their sepias
to fill pages
overlapping
under plastic wrap?
Do they understand
this is
another kind of immortality?

## AT THE JAPANESE GARDEN

Rain washes
the Poetry Stone,
glides over raked white sand
patterns in the stone garden,
making puddles
around the great lantern,
and greens
the mosses into velvet.

The iron water birds
glisten beside the pool
where the almost-moon bridge
stands. Rain rings
on the water speak
to the carp that nudge
algae on the bottom.

At the tea house
stands the dogwood planted
in tears behind a bamboo fence
for delicate Elizabeth
who spoke in the spirit
of haiku and irises, then died.
Friends find there a tryst.

## CHILD'S GIFT

The day the tiger lilies hung
their orange lanterns in rainy woods
the children came to probe fungus
on dead trees and sketch
the lace of maidenhair. Their chatter
trilled with towhees and sparrows,
interrupted riveting woodpeckers.
They intruded the daysleep
of beavers. Small creatures scurried.

> Somewhere far off the guns of war
> are being primed.
> Somewhere out there black flowers,
> nuclear nightshade, wait to burst.

We surrender to the green world,
concerned with the shapes of flowers,
texture of bark, how to heal nettle
sting, rubbing on two elderberry leaves.
And if the sting persists we carry
our minds to the highest tree and leave
it there, until we do not feel the sting
any more. When children grow into pain
will they remember about the highest tree?

## PARTS

Fifty people stood in a great hall
listening to silences.
A guru-like man
in black turtleneck called a signal
to clap hands, each to strike
his own rhythm. Varying cadences
merged into a fabric of sound
like water cascading over rocks
into a tide pool.

The hypnotic rhythms carried fifty
people into an inner stillness.
After the clamor had died down,
we felt the spell break from us
as we were betrayed into speech.
What does one say to a stranger
when retreating to the far wall
for regrouping of kaleidoscopic
fragments? Perhaps no word.

# Chapter VI. BREAKING

by Sam Oakland

## DEJA VU

Golden & orange flashes
now and then a red or silver streak —
Burmese carp
&
their cousins
tread water carefully
through a green-blue channel
beneath
an arched grey stone bridge
near
an ancient teahouse
where
travelers, for centuries,
have paused & shared
the view with ancestors
who passed by
on the same road
earlier.

## IN THE EYE OF THE BEHOLDER

Haunting looks escape dark corners
of forgotten temples
&
forbidden gardens
casting shadows
across
dusty paths unwalked
in recent times.
Westerners of the 80's
falter, stumble,
and fall, once again,
in awe
under the power of
ancient bronze dragons
&
porcelain buddhas
&
the mystery
of the Middle Kingdom.

## ONE MAN, ONE CART, ETERNITY

Piled high with everything imaginable
under South China's boiling sun
homemade carts — a few well-worn planks
on a frame held high
above dirt roads
by an axle with bent wheels —
poke forth
long insistent tongues,
&
harness lean
beautiful fit
old-before-their-time
young men
to an everlasting stream of sweat
from morning to night
year after year.

## THE DUST BIN WOMAN

An old woman irons candy wrappers
and carefully opens and separates
layers of cigarette packages.

Different stacks grow taller.

Tangerine rinds are lined up,
waiting their places,
and litter is brushed aside.

The use-able is squirreled out of
dust bins and spread out
for inspection,

Salvage begins.

It is morning in South China.

The old woman with face tanned
by an uncountable
number of summers

shuffles off,
her loot safe
in two swaying baskets;

they will be full before daybreak.

When the sun comes she will have lived
another whole morning — she will iron
most of the day.

It may be the same tomorrow.

It has been the same before.

## COUPLES

The rim of Banyan Lake, evening.
An iron fence holds back the misdirected.
Two bicycles here and there,
    leaning, unwatched,
    wait together.
Red flames brighten and dim
    small dots of energy
    come alive and then die out.
Smoke, outlines of life,
    quiet words, muffled in shadows.
Sometimes soft sounds of struggle.
The morning will find evidence:
    bent grass, smooth spaces
    where bodies
    have met in cautious touching.
Bamboo groves provide the first shelter.

## 1 NET, 1 MAN, 1 FISH, & A TRIANGLE

Extending from a pole in the right hand
    a fine gage cotton net of many seasons
    stretched into igloo shape over bamboo
    waits patiently, hugging the bottom
    near the bank of the muddy river
    while
    the old Kwangsi fisherman
    reaches to the far left
    &
    begins a rhythmic pattern
    with his triangle.
The semi-circle sweep startles darting fish
    into the quickly raised trap.
One or two tiny captives per try,
    three or four bites at the most.
It will take hours to fill the creel.
It will take creels to fill the family.

## WHITE CATERPILLARS & GREEN SHOOTS

The water buffalo watches
the Hunan farmer
stretch
rolls & rolls of translucent plastic
over
an uncountable
number of bamboo hoops
creating long
graceful
white dragon caterpillars.
Rice grows faster
but
the romantic countryside
of old China
is gone forever,
eaten up by man's invention.

## STANDING ROOM ONLY

Like Norwegian Lemmings*
to the sea
they rush when station gates
crack open —
flooding forward
fast
faster
carrying everything on
the first wave
breaking
to find
a seat, a place,
a corner,
somewhere to lean
on China's
over-burdened trains.

* Small North Europe animals who swarm en mass during migration seasons to the sea coast.

## ROLLING CAR SERVICE

The gleaming white oil clothed tables
    and
    softer white cotton chair covers
    play
    counterpoint to the natural wood
    of the ancient dining car
    while
    a few chosen passengers
    eat
    with painted chopsticks
    from china plates
    and drink Tsingtao export beer
    as
    well-used metal carts
    roll out of the steaming galley
    to feed the rest of the train.

## MORNING EXERCISES

The dutiful passenger
    dashes onto the station platform
    early in the morning
    hoping the train will not restart
    before
    his shadow boxing is over.
Body movements are sweeping
    &
    graceful
    but
    his nose twitches
    &
    his eyes dart anxiously
    between
    the still open door of
    the sleeping car
    &
    the green flag
    in the hand of the signalman.

## THE SLEEPING WAGON

One old railway wagon with a better past
stays in line
and follows the crowd north
carrying sixty sleeping souls
on bunks three high —
bunks a bit too short,
too narrow, too hard
&
too dear —
watched over in the still
moving night
by
green bananas, yellow grapefruit,
&
oranges in swinging nets —
trophies from the trip south.

## THE RED SCARE

Like a flame out of the mouth
of a Wuhan oven at mid-summer
a red sun licks out of Middle Kingdom
heavens
&
begins to devour lands below.
Spring green grass withers & browns,
lakes dry up
&
small fish gasp for air
in the few mud puddles left on earth
as Peking ducks waddle
aimlessly
in thick black muck
like drunken fellow travelers
on one last journey, somewhere.
Turtles gather courage
for a cross country escape
& one very little panda bear
dies in a natural prison.

## ONE MAN'S MUSIC IS ANOTHER MAN'S MEAL

Frogs & peepers
    joined in song
    one spring near my balcony
    where the little stream crossed under
    the road & trickled down
    terraced fields
    to the lake.
I enjoyed the chorus
    coming & going
    each day . .
One noon a geese herd
    brought his flock
    and stayed quite late.
That night was quiet
    &
    so was the next morning
    &
    the morning after that.

## THE ANNUAL VISIT

They come in droves up the dusty path
    to the hillsides
    past angry trucks, jeeps
    & buses blaring out obscenities.
Once a year they gather
    to honor, to remember,
    while the noises of the road cry out
    in a disharmony of sounds
    and compete for attention.
Rank upon rank upon rank
    bearing gifts and memories;
    an almost unending file of humanity
    linking arms with the past.
    They pay respects
    and make way for others.
Firecrackers flash & pop & jabber
    & sputter covering their retreat
    & turn to dust in the place
    where the ashes are kept.

## THE COUNTRY GIRL

The young girl from Kwangsi
countryside,
away from home for the first time,
sat
in awe in the house
of the great Peking Intellectual
spitting sunflower seed shells
in a protective semi-circle
around
the ornately carved claw feet
of an ancient rosewood chair
beneath her,
not noticing all the other guests
using silver dishes
for their droppings.

## ONE PICTURE IS WORTH A THOUSAND WORDS

The roadside entrepreneur
    does his magic in a black box*
    in
    bright sunshine
    and sends happy customers away
    looking at their own images
    in
    white & black
    at arm's length
    trying
    not to put fingerprints
    on
    still wet negative strips
    that fly like tails
    from a dragon kite.

* portable darkroom

## CHINESE AQUADUCTS

Transplanted Roman aquaducts
    spreading
    across
    the dry earth of Shantung Province
    arch upon arch
    keystone in each,
    they lace & tie
    the mountains to the fields.
Which native engineer
    designed
    this conveyance
    that makes
    green spring
    from brown soil?

## NO ONE OVERSLEEPS

Loudspeakers hung from lightpoles
vibrating female voices
singing falsetto

carry long distances

into dormitories.

Flocks of reluctant uniforms

in grey, blue,

&

olive drab

wearing straight black hair

scramble out

& up well worn stone stairs

mumbling, before the bell —

The afternoon nap is over.

Green tiled roofs

like double-ended Viking ships

prows skyward

pierce the heavens.

Spring rains wash

soon empty streets.

## FULL-STOP REQUIRED: BICYCLES ONLY

At every entrance, every exit,
every gate
dipping & bowing
they make some sign,
pretending to touch
pretending to stop
feigning with style.
Dancers at a different pace,
a change of tempo
with practiced legs
saluting
the always watching audience
&
sometimes coming all the way
back down to earth again
before flying quickly on.

## A FORMER GERMAN COLONY

On hills like Rome
    turn-of-the-century manor houses
        flock down through tall evergreens
            to the shores.

Grey rocks appear and disappear
    in uncertain surf,

while

    an empty strand of dazzling white sand

    contrasts with

    the blue of The Yellow Sea &
    the blue of the sky.

Uniformed seagulls float above in formation
    watching strangely shaped humans
        emerge from wooden bathhouses
            near the beach.

A solitary sailboat braves
    near-winter winds

    as the kelp farmer near the quay
    shakes his head in wonder

    and goes back to working his bed.

Dark clouds begin to gather in the north.

**IT'S IN THE WATER***

In a land of mystery
in a land of contradictions
only barbarians**
from The Holy Roman Empire
could leave such a legacy:
a place
where
good beer & good sacred water
are bottled together
to compete in the Chinese marketplace
&
where
both are held in the highest regard.

* An American saying about good beer.

** Tsingtao was a German colony with breweries set up in the 19th century using local holy water from the sacred mountain of Laoshan in Shantung Province.

**THE FLYING TIGERS**

The old Kweilin farmer
    noticing a stranger on the pathway
    between his two rice fields
    grinned & said:
    "they used to land
     right over there
     those flying tigers."
The stranger could only think of
    John Wayne,
    shark-nose planes,
    &
    leather jackets with flags . . .
But the farmer remembered
    the real men,
    the real fighter planes
    &
    the real bombers
    that came to find them all . . . . .

## TSINGTAO CATHEDRAL

The plain black marble cross
    over the entrance
    silent, upright
    rests
    in place still
    but aged & worn now
    with chipped edges
    from recent years, recent weather.
Fallen rocks and bits of stone
    spent in anger
    lay
    clinging to the ledge
    beneath
    as young workmen scale her
    twin towers & new architects
    search the country for stained
    glass.
Winds of change blow warmer
    as spring edges near.

**ABOUT THE AUTHOR, Penny Avila**

Penny Avila was born at Castleton Avenue on Staten Island, New York, on October 10, 1911. She served as Assistant Air Raid Warden of Staten Island during World War II. She married Bert Avila and moved to Oregon in 1953. She began writing in 1968. Her work included short stories, profiles, poetry, and book reviews. She was the Oregonian's Poetry Editor for many years.

Ms. Avila is the author of *KALEIDOSCOPE IN A SIFTING OF ASHES,* 1982, and *THE PEACOCK SPREADS HIS TAIL,* forthcoming from India, 1985. Ms. Avila's poems have appeared in *WRITER'S DIGEST; NORTHWEST MAGAZINE — THE OREGONIAN; RAINDANCE; WILLAMETTE WEEK; BLACK WILLOW; BLUE UNICORN; POETRY MAGAZINE; LINCOLN NEWS GUARD; A LONG TERM UNDERGROUND PLAN; WORLD POETRY 1 — POETRY AMERICAS,* Madras, India, Dr. Krishna Srinivas, Editor; *CONFLUENCE,* a Portland Anthology/Portland Poetry Festival; *FIFTH WORLD CONGRESS OF POETS ANTHOLOGY; THE PEN WOMAN.* The poem, *Spectator Sport on an Olympic High* was read at the Science Congress of the 1984 Olympics.

Ms. Avila received a Doctorate Honorarium from The World Academy of Arts & Culture Congress, 1985, Madras, India, and is a member of the Congress. She is currently Oregon's Ambassador of Poetry and the President of Oregon State Poetry Association. She is a member of Willamette Writers and National Penwomen's Association. Ms. Avila started the Portland Zoo Children's Poetry Contest. She resides with her husband, Bert, in Lake Oswego, Oregon, and is the mother of a daughter, Berl Avreanne.

**ABOUT THE AUTHOR, Lawson Fusao Inada**

Lawson Fusao Inada was born on May 26, 1938, in Fresno, California. Mr. Inada is the author of *BEFORE THE WAR,* 1971, the first book of poetry by an Asian-American to be published by a major firm, and an editor of the Asian-American anthology, *AIIIEEEEE!,* Doubleday, 1976; *THE BIG AIIIEEEEE!,* Howard University Press, forthcoming, 1985. He is under contract to Howard University for a book on the American concentration camp experience. Mr. Inada's poetry has appeared in collections by Avon, Bantam, Crowell, Dell, Doubleday, Grove, Harcourt, Houghton Mifflin, Macmillan, New Directions, Random House, and Scott Foresman. He is part of the *ENCYCLOPAEDIA BRITANNICA* filmstrip series on American Literature. He is the subject of a documentary film, *I TOLD YOU SO* sponsored by HEW and the Los Angeles Public Schools. In January, 1980, he was invited to read at the White House for "A SALUTE TO POETRY AND AMERICAN POETS." His study of Japanese-American literature, "Of Place and Displacement," appears in *THREE AMERICAN LITERATURES,* Modern Language Association, 1982. He is serving on the Task Force on Racism and Bias in Education for the National Council of Teachers of English. In 1984, he received the Excellence in Teaching Award from The Oregon State Board of Higher Education.

Mr. Inada is now Professor of English at Southern Oregon State College at Ashland, Oregon. He is married to Janet and they have two sons, Miles and Lowell.

**ABOUT THE AUTHOR, Joanne Stevens Sullivan**

Joanne Stevens Sullivan was born at Main Street in the heart of downtown Milwaukie, Oregon, on March 12, 1937. She grew up in a large family that had strong Norwegian traditions. In 1955, she married and became the mother of five children: Steven Michael, Julie Carol, Melanie Ruth, Jerry L. and Ross William. She became a single parent in 1975, and in 1977, married Don Sullivan, a college instructor. A writer of thirty years, Ms. Sullivan combined college classes and writing poetry, finishing her book, *ORCHIDS IN THE SAND* in 1984. Ms. Sullivan is currently a graphic artist and book designer in Portland, Oregon, where she resides with her husband.

One hundred poems comprise *ORCHIDS IN THE SAND.* Ms. Sullivan's poems have appeared in *RHAPSODY!,* Spring Edition, 1984, Fall/Winter Edition, 1984; *NORTHWEST MAGAZINE — THE OREGONIAN: THE ENTERPRISE COURIER; THE PRINT; THE BULLETIN;* and *ARCHER;* Ms. Sullivan received an award for the poem, "Mother's Vow," from the Oregon Association of American Mothers in 1984.

Ms. Sullivan is past chairman of the Art Review Committee for Clackamas Community College, has been a judge for the Portland Zoo Children's Contest, has served as Historian for the Oregon State Poetry Association and is a member of Willamette Writers.

**ABOUT THE AUTHOR, Vern Rutsala**

Vern Rutsala was born on February 5, 1934, in McCall, Idaho. He graduated from Reed College and the University of Iowa Writer's Workshop. He is currently Professor of English at Lewis & Clark College.

Mr. Rutsala wrote *THE WINDOW,* published by Wesleyan University Press, 1964; *LAMENTS,* published by New Rivers Press, 1975; *THE JOURNEY BEGINS,* published by the University of Georgia Press, 1976, Copyright Vern Rutsala; *PARAGRAPHS,* published by Wesleyan University Press, 1978; *WALKING HOME FROM THE ICEHOUSE,* 1981, Copyright Vern Rutsala;

Mr. Rutsala received two National Endowment for the Arts Fellowships in 1974 and 1979, and the Guggenheim Fellowship in 1981. He resides with his wife, Joan, and children, Kirsten, Matthew and David in Portland, Oregon.

## ABOUT THE AUTHOR, Anita Lewisohn Hamm

Anita Lewisohn Hamm attended Marylhurst College, Eastern Oregon College of Education, Chaffey College and earned her Master of Arts degree in Arts and Letters from Portland State University. Ms. Hamm has been a journalist, teacher of creative writing in Portland Public Schools, Author in the Schools, and is a prize winning poet. Ms. Hamm wrote *POCKETS OF TIME,* Samara Publications, 1982, a collection of poems, and she is the author of three children's books: *LISA AND THE RAINDROPS,* 1980; *LEAF IT TO ME*; 1980; *LISA IN SUGARLAND, A CHILD'S BOOK OF NUTRITION TO BE DIGESTED BEFORE EATING,* 1978, Samara Publications.

Ms. Hamm has been Education Director at Tryon Creek State Park for the past eight years, a position that combines her love for children and nature. Originally from Pensacola, Florida, Ms. Hamm now lives in Milwaukie, Oregon, with her husband, Elmer. Their children are Charles, James, Robert and Elaine.

Ms. Hamm is a past president of the Oregon State Poetry Association and is a member of Willamette Writers. In 1983 she was nominated for Mother of the Year and was named Merit Mother by the Oregon Association of American Mothers. She is State Literary Chairman for the Oregon Association of American Mothers, 1984/85.

**ABOUT THE AUTHOR, Sam Oakland**

Sam-Adolf Sjürsen Oakland was born on Mulberry Street during a snow storm at teatime in St. Joseph, Missouri on St. Patrick's Day in 1934. The only son of a Norwegian poet/engineer and a Scots/Irish/Welsh governess, he now lives and writes in Oregon. Mr. Oakland is married to Sara, and they have two children, Sasha Kari and Steven Anders.

Mr. Oakland studied at Michigan State University and has held Fulbrights to Finland and Rome. Recently, he spent a year as Visiting Writer and Lecturer in The Peoples Republic of China. *LOVE BLOOMS UNDER THE BLACK UMBRELLAS* is Mr. Oakland's book being published, 1985, in Peking, China, in a bilingual edition in Chinese and English. Chapter VI, "Breaking," of *BETWEEN RAINDROPS* is poetry written while Mr. Oakland was living in China, roaming the cities and countryside. Mr. Oakland's prose writings have appeared in many languages published abroad, including Chinese, Hebrew, Macedonian, Norwegian and Serbian. He is overseas editor of *THE INTERNATIONAL PORTLAND REVIEW,* which publishes prose and poetry in original languages, along with English translations.

**Mica Publishing Company**
**"Between Raindrops"**
**P. O. Box 14931**
**Portland, Oregon 97214**